Heart Chakra Cleansing

A Guide to Heart Chakra Meditation and Heart Chakra Healing

by Priya Chevallier

Table of Contents

Introduction

Are you unhappy? Feeling lonely? Having problems with relationships?

Your heart chakra may be blocked or misaligned. The heart chakra is one of the seven major energy centers in the body, and if this particular chakra is not open or balanced, it can result in being unable to connect with other people on a deeper level. As a result, relationships can be hard to maintain, and it often leads to an emotional pain that just won't go away on its own.

The heart chakra has a lot to do with your ability to love, forgive, and let go of resentment. People with a balanced and open chakra have the ability to open their hearts to other people, to show compassion, to give love, and to accept love. If you are holding onto anger, resentment, and painful memories, then your heart chakra is probably blocked and off-balance. This results in relationship problems, trouble connecting with and committing to others, and the inability to truly enjoy meaningful relationships. So if you're yearning for emotional and spiritual growth, or are simply tired of having a broken heart, then perhaps it is time you looked into the current state of your heart chakra.

This book is designed to help you open and balance your heart chakra, and to teach you effective meditation practices that will help clear and align the Anahata, your fourth chakra. Once you have a balanced heart chakra, you can connect with others on a deeper level and you'll be able to release negative emotions such as anger, jealousy, pride, and envy, among other things. You'll be able to open and share your heart with other people, relieving yourself of any emotional baggage you may have been carrying through the years. With an open and clear hear chakra, you can rise above all negative emotions and achieve a higher state of consciousness. You'll be able to forgive people that have wronged you… but most importantly, you'll be able to forgive yourself. It's never too late to start taking care of your heart chakra, so let's get started now. With an open and balanced heart chakra, you can experience and enjoy immense love in your life, in order to become whole again and attain the inner peace that you so deeply desire.

Chapter 1: Getting to Know the Heart Chakra

In Sanskrit, the heart chakra is referred to as the "Anahata" chakra. In the body, it can be found in your chest area – where the heart is also located – and in the chakra system, it is situated right at the middle of the seven energy centers. The heart chakra plays a very essential role, as it connects the upper and lower chakras to bring together spiritual and physical energies. Love, connection, forgiveness, and compassion are directly related to the heart chakra. The colors that represent this power center are green and pink.

On a physical level, an open and balanced heart chakra will support healthy connections and relationships. On a spiritual level, the fourth chakra allows people to let go of any feelings of loneliness, and helps you to feel that you're a part of something bigger and that you belong. This leads to having a sense of inner peace. Every person must strive to attain a balanced heart chakra because when we have this, we are able to forgive, trust, love, and feel compassion for others. People who have a clear Anahata chakra are non-judgmental and are more accepting of others. They can easily make friends and are close to nature. Due to the inner peace that they exude, their presence often gives a calming effect to other people. When it comes to physical health, a balanced heart chakra can result in a healthy respiratory and circulatory system.

The heart chakra is the center for inner peace and self-acceptance. The lesson that one should learn of the fourth energy center is forgiveness. When we repress bad memories, the heart chakra can become clogged. Child abuse victims and those that suffer from traumatic experiences can have physical ailments and carry emotional pain with them even after many years have passed. Separation, abandonment, divorce, and death are only a few of the experiences that can have a very strong effect on the emotional state of a person, and can even cause the person to develop illnesses. When a person is suffering from emotional pain, it can be very easy to simply hold on to anger. However, doing this will only cause the heart chakra to be blocked, and this leads to physical, emotional, mental, and spiritual ailments. Opening the heart chakra allows the release of all painful memories, and allows us to forgive those who may have caused us pain in the past. Only then can inner peace and good health be achieved.

In some cases, the heart chakra can close or shut down, and that leads to the person's inability to love, trust, feel compassion, and accept others as well as himself or herself. With a closed heart chakra, you will have a hard time building connections, staying in a long-term relationship, and will have a sense of being alone even if you're already in a loving relationship, with others around you who care about you. On the other hand, an overactive heart chakra can make a person long for the approval of others in order to feel happy. An imbalance in the heart chakra on either side of the spectrum can lead to poor physical, emotional, mental, and spiritual health. Illnesses associated with a blocked or imbalanced heart chakra include: breast cancer, heart disease, respiratory illnesses, allergies, and depression.

Chapter 2: Opening and Balancing Your Heart Chakra

In order to attain inner peace and enjoy meaningful and long-term relationships in life, the heart chakra must be open and balanced. The heart chakra is the center of unconditional love, honesty, empathy, and self-acceptance.

Opening your heart can be as simple as letting go of anger, resentment, envy, and jealousy. When you are able to forgive the people that have wronged you, you are on your way to having an open your heart chakra.

Here is an exercise to help you assess the condition of your heart chakra. Let's start by asking yourself these questions, and being brutally honest with yourself in answering each:

- "Is there anger in my heart right now?"

- "Am I harboring jealousy and envy in my heart?"

- "Is there someone that I need to forgive?"

- "Do I need to ask the forgiveness of someone?"

- "What emotional wounds do I have?"

- "Are my emotional wounds healing or am I keeping it fresh?"

- "Are there bad memories that I need to let go?"

After answering these questions as honestly as you can, you'll have a clearer picture of any unresolved feelings that you might be carrying in your heart. And as soon as you acknowledge the existence of all these negative emotions, you can be on your way to reopening your heart chakra.

The heart chakra has much to do with loving yourself first. People cannot have the experience of truly loving another person until they learn to love themselves. We've all heard that before, right? Well, that's because it's absolutely true. Being in touch with the fourth chakra requires determination and practice, so let the love start within yourself. Love yourself, and you'll soon be able to give unconditional love to others. Keep in mind that the love you give will find its way back to you.

Practical Ways to Open and Balance Your Heart Chakra

Love Yourself

Accept who you are. Love the person that you are. Don't compare yourself to others, or wish that you were another person. That attitude is very unhealthy, and can block your heart chakra. Instead, look at your positive and negative attributes, and accept them. Once you accept all of yourself, then you will be truly happy. Take care of your body, heart, mind, and spirit. When things don't go your way, don't be too hard on yourself. Accept your limitations and do the best you can to learn from your experiences.

Show Kindness All the Time

Some say that a random act of kindness is what every person should give. However, it is best to be kind all the time. Being kind is a conscious choice you can choose to make. Do everything with kindness in your heart. Choose to be kind. Remember that all acts of kindness are rewarded, and that whatever you give out there in the Universe, whether it is rudeness or kindness, will eventually find its way back to you.

Enjoy Nature

If you spend most of your time cooped up in your office or in your home, perhaps it is time you put on those sneakers and go for a walk. Breathe in the fresh air, and open your ears to the sound of the wind and the birds. Use this time to connect with nature, and enjoy the feeling of belonging and being a part of this universe.

Be Grateful

When people focus on the hurt and the pain, it can be hard to be grateful. However, once you start forgiving and letting go of bad memories, you can start seeing all the little things in your life that you should be thankful for. Also, reminding yourself to be grateful for all the good things will allow you to focus on the positive things in life, instead of holding onto anger or pain.

Contact Old Friends

Getting in touch with old friends is a good way to open a blocked heart chakra. There might be some unresolved issues out there between you and your friends, and this may be a good chance to resolve them. Also, you can benefit from reconnecting with people that truly care for you, and experience the happiness that comes along with that.

Be Around Small Children

Small children exude goodness, and don't harbor any negative emotions like anger, envy, or jealousy. Being around children can open your eyes to innocence, giving without expecting, and the simple joys in life.

Surround Yourself in Green and Pink

If you have an office or a cubicle at work, place the colors of the heart chakra in it. You can also decorate your bedroom in either green or pink to help open your fourth chakra.

Get a Dog

Dogs are often associated to the topic of unconditional love. These gentle creatures are loyal to their masters, and will often demonstrate signs of unconditional love even if they are neglected. Unconditional love is one of the characteristics needed in order to have an open chakra.

Help Others

There are certainly numerous ways that you can do this. The easiest way would be to go to a homeless shelter and offer your services. Helping others opens a blocked heart chakra, because you will feel be able to feel empathy and selflessness when helping others in need.

Use Essential Oils That Fuel the Heart Chakra

Essential oils like jasmine, sandalwood, chamomile, and rose can help to open and balance the heart chakra. Scented candles in these scents can also be used in aromatherapy.

Connect with Family

Call your mom, talk to your dad, sister, brother, and other relatives. Being around the family can give a person positive and loving vibes. Family members generally support each other, and even when words aren't used, the unconditional love for each other exudes naturally from each family member.

Recreation

Don't allow yourself to look back at the painful memories and feel the pain again. Instead, find ways to entertain yourself like reading a book, watching a heartening movie, or hanging out with friends. Cheer yourself up.

Love Unconditionally

This can be very hard to do, but unconditional love is the best way to obtain a healthy heart chakra. Love without asking for anything in return. Love because you can give love and are capable of love. Love freely.

Throw Away Anger, Jealousy, and Hate

These emotions are very destructive, and harboring these in your heart can be a very unhealthy practice. It also creates a blockage in your heart chakra. So chuck out these negative emotions, and enjoy an open and balanced chakra. In addition, if you want to realign and clear your heart chakra, you cannot claim to love some people and hate others. In order for the heart chakra to be fully open and balanced, one should be able to love fully and remove all negative feelings inside of them.

Practice Yoga (or at least try it if you haven't!)

Yoga is a great way to open and balance the fourth chakra. There are yoga poses that specifically target the chest area with the main goal of balancing the heart chakra.

Meditate

Meditation allows people to focus and channel their energies. It can also help a person to calm down and release any bad energy that has become trapped in their body.

Use Crystals and Gemstones

Crystals have been used for a long time to heal the body, heart, mind, and spirit. Wearing green and pink gemstones or crystals such as jade, peridot, emerald, rose quartz, pink diamonds, and malachite are helpful in balancing the heart chakra.

Chapter 3: Heart Chakra Meditation

At times, you may feel that you just can't connect with the people around you or that it's difficult to feel the love that should be flowing all around you. Meditation allows you to listen to the heart beats of those who care for you, and will make it easier for you to connect with them.

A Heart Chakra Meditation

- Lie down in a flat surface. Make sure that you are comfortable. Close your eyes.

- Take a deep breath and then slowly exhale. Do this two more times.

- This time, breathe in and place your arms around your body, giving yourself a hug. And as you breathe out, stretch your arms to your sides and allow them to rest on the floor.

- Lying on your back, feel your vulnerability as a person but also allow yourself to feel your connection to the earth.

- Lie still and take a few more deep breaths, but always exhaling slowly.

- Keeping your eyes closed, visualize that you are releasing all negative energies as you exhale.

- With every exhalation, allow yourself to let go of all stagnant and harmful energies such as greed, anger, hate, and jealousy.

- And when you inhale, visualize the new and positive life energies flowing throughout your body.

- Listen to the rhythm of your breathing. This is the beating of your heart. Every beat is significant because new energy enters your body. Every heart beat should remind you that you are capable of giving love and receiving love.

- Allow your body and mind to feel calm.

- This time as you breathe in, let the love that is flowing freely around you to enter your heart.

- As you exhale, send out the love that you have and feel for the people around you.

- Allow the love to fill your body.

- Lie down there for a bit. Use this time to cleanse your heart of any fear, anger, hate, envy, and resentment.

- Now, when you are ready, slowly open your eyes and share the love that you feel to your family, friends, and special someone.

- Spread the love that you feel in your heart to other people as well and receive any love that comes your way.

Chapter 4: Rose Quartz Meditation

Crystals and gemstones in green and pink are helpful in achieving a clear and balanced heart chakra. The rose quartz is a pink crystal used for heart chakra meditation. It is widely recognized as "the love stone", because it carries energies that promote unconditional love, peace, nourishment, compassion, forgiveness, comfort, tenderness, and healing. The rose quartz sends out gentle vibrations that help open and balance the heart chakra. Wearing a rose quartz in your body or placing it around you will give you a feeling of self-worth and inner peace.

The rose quartz meditation will help you clear out a blocked heart chakra. The location of the heart chakra is not an accident; it plays a very significant role, which is to connect the lower chakras with the upper chakras. A blocked heart chakra can affect the flow of energies from one chakra to another. Therefore, it is important to keep the heart chakra open all the time to ensure balance in all seven of the major chakras.

Here is a simple rose quartz meditation that will allow you to re-center quickly. You can do this in your home or in your office during your break time because it will only take 10 minutes.

A Rose Quartz Meditation

- Lie down in a comfortable position.

- Place a rose quartz in your chest and hold it in place with both hands.

- Close your eyes and inhale deeply. Exhale slowly.

- Place both arms on your sides and just relax.

- As you breathe in and breathe out, calm your mind by focusing on the sound of your breathing. Block out any other sound that you hear around you and just concentrate on your breathing.

- Allow yourself to feel the gentle vibrations coming out from the rose quartz. Allow the vibrations to reach your heart chakra.

- Visualize that the energy emitted from the rose quartz is a pink ball of light that is now coursing through your power centers.

- Allow the pink light to move over your body, beginning from your toes and going up to your head. Visualize a pink light now enveloping your whole body.

- Feel the love, compassion, and forgiveness surrounding you. Feel calm and peaceful.

- Enjoy this state of love and peace for a few minutes.

- When you are ready, place both of your hands on the rose quartz in your chest and slowly inhale and exhale.

- Open your eyes, and carry the peace and love that you felt during the meditation with you for the rest of the day.

Chapter 5: Forgiveness Meditation

Hurtful experiences have a tendency to remain in our hearts and minds, even after many years have passed. Some people heal their wounds by forgiving, while others keep their wounds fresh by reliving the painful past experiences. It's so much easier to be angry than to forgive. However, keeping anger, hate, and resentment in our hearts can cause an imbalanced heart chakra. These negative energies can get trapped in the blockage and could potentially become stagnant energies. As a result of a blocked heart chakra, new life energy is prevented from continuously flowing in and out of the chakras and the body. Forgiveness means accepting the past and any painful experiences that came along with it. It requires letting go of the anger that we feel towards people that have hurt us.

The forgiveness meditation allows the stagnant energy of anger, hate, and resentment to be released from the body. It helps the person to forgive, and let go of a painful past. The forgiveness meditation opens a choked heart chakra. Before doing the forgiveness meditation, it is important that you feel comfortable and open to the idea of finally letting go of your anger.

A Forgiveness Meditation

This forgiveness meditation takes 45 minutes, so be sure to find a spot where you won't be disturbed. Wear comfortable clothes and you can even take a hot shower before starting with the meditation to make sure that you can relax physically and mentally. Before starting the meditation, you'll need to create affirmations. It's up to you if you want to come up with your own but you can also use these:

Affirmations:

"I am a strong person."
"I am in control of my life."
"I am safe."
"I am loved."
"I accept what happened."
"I forgive those that have hurt me."
"I free myself of anger and hate."
"I am happy."

Steps:

1. Sit comfortably in a chair. Rest your arms in the arm rest, stretch your legs right in front of you, and relax your feet.

2. Inhale deeply and exhale slowly. Calm you mind and heart. Relax your body. Repeat inhaling deeply and exhaling slowly until you feel that you are calm.

3. When you are comfortable and ready, recall a hurtful past experience that still bothers you today. If there are many, pick the one that troubles you the most. Most of the time, your mind will naturally single out the most upsetting issue.

4. At this point, your mind and body can become involuntarily tensed again, but try to maintain a calm mind and a relaxed body by breathing in and breathing out rhythmically.

5. Saying your affirmations.

As you breathe in deeply, say this affirmation in your mind: "I am a strong person."

As you exhale slowly, say this affirmation in your mind: "I am in control of my life."

Inhale: "I am safe."

Exhale: "I am loved."

Inhale: "I accept what happened."

Exhale: "I forgive those that have hurt me."

Inhale: "I free myself of anger and hate."

Exhale: "I am happy."

6. You can say as many affirmations as you need. When you feel ready to proceed, breathe in and breathe out peacefully.

7. Now start going over the events in your painful experience. Only do this if you feel ready and comfortable. If at any point, you feel that you are not yet ready to proceed, don't force yourself. Instead, you can stop at Step Number 6. You can proceed to the next step when you are ready.

8. Go over the events that led to your painful experience. Be careful not to put any blame on yourself or on other people. Just look at the events as objectively as you can.

***The forgiveness meditation requires people to face their past, not deny it. It helps us to release bad memories, not repress them. Therefore, going over the painful event can be helpful as it helps the person to acknowledge the pain and accept that it really happened. By doing so, he can be on his way to healing.

9. After carefully going through your painful experience, acknowledge your pain and the person that has hurt you. You should also accept any wrongdoing on your part.

10. Now, your goal is to release the anger and the pain that you are feeling. Visualize yourself carrying a big, black, heavy rock. You are walking around with it, your shoulders bent and your arms weary. The rock is your anger and pain. What relief it can be to just let go of this burden! Inhale deeply and as you exhale, visualize yourself finally letting go of this heavy

burdensome rock. You feel immediate relief as you let go of the rock and as you watch it fall on the ground. Now, you stand straight and continue walking, feeling light as a bird. You look forward to your journey and never look back at the rock you left behind you.

11. Inhale deeply and exhale slowly. Feel the peace and lightheartedness of having let go of your anger and pain.

12. When you feel ready, open your eyes and strive to live a life free of anger and hate.

Forgiveness does not require an active participation from the offending party. You can forgive that person who has hurt you even when he does not ask for your forgiveness. Keep in mind that when you forgive, it must be unconditional. You don't need the other person to beg for your forgiveness or to acknowledge that he has caused you pain. You need to forgive those who hurt you because you want to be free of hate and anger. You want to move on. When you forgive, you are releasing the negative energies in your body and clearing up your heart chakra. A lot of people refuse to forgive, and wait in vain for the offending party to come to them first and ask for forgiveness. And when that does not happen, they

34

suffer all their lives. So forgive unconditionally, and experience the feeling of being truly free.

Chapter 6: Healing by Letting Go of Regrets

Regrets are unresolved feelings that people carry with them wherever they go for many years. Everybody has done things that they later on wish they hadn't. No one is perfect, and mistakes are what make us human. And while there are people who never give their past mistakes another thought, there are those that have come to peace with it. Nevertheless, there are individuals who cannot accept their past shortcomings and wallow in misery all their lives.

When we regret a past behavior or decision, it often accompanies a wish that it could be undone. Regrets lead to denial and the tendency to blame in order to alleviate the pain that one may be suffering from. The person may blame themselves or others. In order to achieve inner peace, we need to accept the fact that things will not always go the way we want them to. Bad things will happen such as accidents, death, and failures. All of this is a part of life, and are necessary to keep balance in our Universe. By not accepting this, we prevent healing and don't allow ourselves to experience real happiness.

Many of man's regrets have something to do with material things. However, lasting happiness can only be attained when we learn to disassociate ourselves with material wealth. The more we become attached to earthly riches, the more unhappy we become. True happiness is found within ourselves. A mother who has chosen to quit her career in order to be a stay-at-home mom should be happy of her decision and not spend every day regretting it. Jobs can be found and money can be earned but time with your kids as they grow up is priceless. People can find true happiness when they look for it inside themselves and not in their bank accounts, inside their garage, or in their relationships.

Regretting our past actions and decisions is a form of denial. We reject the responsibility that comes with our actions and as a result we blame ourselves and those around us. Regrets lead to a life of suffering. We constantly go back to a situation that we cannot change, so we just cause ourselves and other people fresh pain every time. Regrets allow us and those around us to become trapped in a life of suffering. The key is to let go of regrets in order to free yourself and those around you. Stop blaming yourself or others. Accept responsibility for your actions, behavior, and decisions.

Keep in mind that the heart chakra represents compassion, forgiveness, and love. Loving yourself means accepting your mistakes. Before you can love others, you need to be able to love yourself. Forgive yourself of your mistakes by showing compassion to others. Holding on to regret and denial will block the heart chakra, and has the potential to cause prolonged suffering. Heal your heart chakra by accepting responsibility for your actions, accepting the events that happened in your life, and accepting that you cannot change what is already done.

Conclusion

As people become busier with their families, careers, earning more money, and collecting material wealth, many have become disengaged from their power centers. Very few people today have any knowledge about the seven chakras and the things they represent. People suffer from all sorts of physical, emotional, mental, and spiritual ailments without knowing that all of these could be the result of a blocked chakra.

An open and balanced heart chakra allows a person to find inner peace, experience true happiness, show compassion, forgive and trust. People's inability to empathize with others and to build meaningful relationships can be a sign of a blocked or imbalanced heart chakra.

Opening, balancing, and healing the heart chakra is the only way to have more meaningful and long-term relationships with other people. When you feel that you have become disconnected to your family, friends, and to the Universe, it's time to examine the health of your heart chakra. If you want to connect with people on a deeper level and enjoy physical, emotional, mental, and spiritual health, then work to keep your heart chakra always open and balanced. Good luck!

Finally, I'd like to thank you for purchasing this book! If you enjoyed it or found it helpful, I'd greatly appreciate it if you'd take a moment to leave a review on Amazon. Thank you!

Made in the
USA
Middletown, DE